THE UNDERSTUDY'S HANDBOOK

STEVEN LEYVA

THE
UNDERSTUDY'S
HANDBOOK

• 2020 JEAN FELDMAN POETRY PRIZE WINNER •

Washington Writers' Publishing House
Washington, D.C.

COVER DESIGN by Andrew Sargus Klein
BOOK LAYOUT by Barbara Shaw
AUTHOR PHOTO by Chris Hartlove

Library of Congress Cataloging-in-Publication Data
Names: Leyva, Steven, 1982- author.
Title: The understudy's handbook / Steven Leyva.
Description: Washington, D.C. : Washington Writers Publishing House, [2020]
  | Summary: "THE UNDERSTUDY'S HANDBOOK is a collection of
  beautifully detailed, emotionally lush poems that comprise a portrait of a life, a
  bi-racial life, an American life. These are smart, evocative poems that invite the
  heart and prime the head to reconcile the intricacies of our individual lives
  with the history that has brought us all to this moment in America"—
  Provided by publisher.
Identifiers: LCCN 2020027886 | ISBN 9781941551226 (paperback)
Subjects: LCGFT: Poetry.
Classification: LCC PS3612.E997 U54 2020 | DDC 811/.6—dc23
LC record available at https://lccn.loc.gov/2020027886

Printed in the United States of America

WASHINGTON WRITERS' PUBLISHING HOUSE
P. O. Box 15271
Washington, D.C. 20003

FOR MY BROTHER

CONTENTS

1.

INSIDE THE MOUTH OF A TRUMPET

"It has to be living, to learn the speech of the place."
—WALLACE STEVENS, "OF MODERN POETRY"

"It is not a question of who is the strongest, but what form of life is the strongest."
—PAUL ROBESON, "THE NEW IDEALISM"

• PRIMER •

There's no New
Orleans, only the pauses between parades.

The city christens
its own, each palm leaf brushing our esplanade

a wet
aspergillum. You will be known

here as a gargoyle
knows each inch of stone

it sleeps in
but cannot wipe its tears.

What has all this
iron wrought? Our family intoning

Zydeco means
the accordion's broken back,

means another
fiddle's whip over catgut,

means there
is a balcony for everyone

to die on.
What is French about these quarters

is exile
all gardens to the backyard—son

remember
to tell your sons. What whispers

in the weary
ear endlessly come here taste

and taste
is an inability to sustain innocence.

No, not quite;
something like feathers plucked from a mask.

• INAMORATA •

O Nola, O old magic
       city the arc of your crescent
             is the same as my mama's

curled lip   I watch
       from behind
             a scrim of hot breath

and early zydeco
       in the evening rises
             a dance you make me dance

until the end
       until a limp
             is left in my right leg

and a funk in the other
       Nola when your bounce
             leaps from speakers

comes the great gyrate
       the whole line
             all heredity backing it up

mama and them rise
       every 9th ward cousin
             wants you thick Nola

drunk uncles crown
       & coke sip
              bring an elastic lust

to every syllable
       "bay-bae" drawn out
              like an aroused cock

a trombone slide   Damn Girl

where'd you sleep
       last night? In the pines?
              Nola you fat and fine

the quick-quick-slow
       that repeats
              like being sick and tired

of being sick
       and tired or late again
              on last week's rent

dance   dance worn out
       limbs and feet
              don't fail me

Nola where'd you sleep
        last night when the storm
                began its wet dream?

• CREOLITE I •

Mist on the marshlands of the tongue.
Here we say *store* and *flow* rhyme. Contrarians.

Born into the family of auto-antonyms we *cleave*
any countersign, any accent, *bolt* to the speakeasy door:

Do you belong? Candor. Born in a basket
of idiom. Go down Moses, cleave the sea

that first taught us neither its great hexameters
nor its plain iambs. Low tide, low parish, low chariot

swing and swing. Carry us. Lightning.
Help us to conjure another homeland. The most specific

pain of exile is boredom, heavy as the humidity,
which always hangs like a carcass of wind in Louisiana.

The earth inside your skull, America across your face,
the South chapping your lips. Mist on the marshlands of the tongue.

• BOY GESTURING OVER
THE LONDON AVE CANAL •

Tongue stuck out, licking a paycheck
worth of icing from a Swiss Cake.
Not the country, mind you, but the confectionery
on Orleans Street. Then the lapping of a few cents
of wet bliss from a cool cup, your neighbor
Tela hocked from her Frigidaire.
Every mouth on the block red as a teacher's pen.

Black tires, black sneaker soles on the face of Robert E. Lee
Blvd. like the dot in a domino, Big Six, the boss spinner,
slapping a table. That's you. The summer's slow pleasure
pulled out like a sleeper sofa, or how the cross
bar of memory impresses on a chest. Juveniles, we
were all Juveniles, ha. No one would deny us I-10
plunging across the city's abdomen like a cesarean scar.

• A ROOM WITH 5 ON REPEAT •
for J. Barrow

It was the year that could not be abbreviated:

2000. Houston. Either the Hot Boys
had managed to take over, or the flaming sword

guarding Eden was out for a walk. You loved Lenny Kravitz
more than God, or any bounce-music from my birth city,

though your mother was Creole, and had we been undressing
to some early Jelly Roll Morton, she might have smiled

before her chiffon mid-heel pump smacked my cheek. She wasn't
home listening to Lenny sing "I Belong to You." Our errant

touching on the couch, our shy fellatio, the mime
work our thighs made to music, felt meager

among the silence we left in the air like overripe fruit. Our gestures:
mine toward the door, yours toward the living room's mess,

both begging the other *don't make me say it*. We can't be
the only animals that blush or ask forgiveness

or plead with a sword of flames for more.

• EAR HUSTLE •

Get down to the smallest birthright
I cannot claim: say beignets
and doesn't the stutter of hot oil start
to sizzle on the small plates of memory?

Faces powdered with sugar, no thought
to whose ancestors cut which cane, sing
a hymn of "mmm, mmm, mmm."
Jackson Square hangs its portraits

on the iron gates. And who can hold a horn
note as long as the midday sun? Look up
from that small plate and café
au lait, and see the bent levees

of language I cannot break. I will shame
every shibboleth. And every house is lifted
like a paused rapture. This cruelty and more
fries the Godhead in lard. Pour me a cup

of chicory. A saxophone player cuts a canal
through the breakfast din, playing Tank
and the Bangas *I gotta make a quick decision*
about how often I can be rescued.

Neither I nor my children will ever ride
the roller coasters at Jazzland
where a sign still hangs as it does in the heavens:
will open after storm.

• A BOONDOCK •

Lisa was the first girl in my life
I asked to dance. I mean, a brass band
was playing early jump blues, not a Louis

Jordan situation, but, you know, the Andrew
Sisters, bugle boy and company B, that business.
Anyway, we were a shave under nine years old,

two hearing kids in an American Sign Language
performance group. And when we were done
signing the lyrics to "God Bless America,"

and after the polite applause of donors
circled back into olives drowning in gin,
the dance floor opened. I asked Lisa Colaco

(she loved to say like Cola Company)
to dance, sheepishly, looking an inch above
my glasses, thinking what would it be

to gently press my brown cheek to one
of her freckles. I'll be dammed if my desires
will ever be that simple again.

Her father was a Catholic from India.
She had his features and dark
hair, but her mother's Nebraskan

complexion. I remember being afraid
for no reason and my hand was shaking
like I was signing "applause," when she

put it on her hip, lassoed my neck
and we spun. I didn't know a waltz
from a Roger Rabbit. All I could think

is scarecrow, Michael Jackson, I mean
imitate an ease on down the road.
We rocked these blue as Skylite t-shirts

decorated with hand prints. A fundraising
situation for *Be an Angel,* this NGO founded
by Lisa's family. My mama must've known it

was gonna be one of those fly in a bowl
of milk moments so she insisted my pants
rest above my navel, shirt tucked, Vaseline

like YWHW's own glory across my forehead.
Call me Moses at the foot of Sinai. My tablets:
a pair of left feet. Just kidding. I was Gregory

Hines in a Harlem night, and if there was a golden
calf, Lisa and I were it. When Lisa moved
I moved and just like that we knew

we'd never see a promised land. Instead of stones
the donors threw their eyebrows in the air
forgetting how colorblind they'd been before gin.

• ETHEL COOKING BÉCHAMEL •

"I'm not gonna tell what it is till after you done cooked it."
—*Aunt Ethel,* The Colored Museum *by Charles C. Wolfe*

1.

Not the roux as fact, but the new white roux.
A rhizome of Tabasco in the pan, gas stove
lit: butter & milk blended like funk slough
in a dance hall. Low heat for centuries.

Cook the books. All of it. This is from scratch
& memory. Take it like a slow drag.
Sauce won't brown when whipped gradually or
quick. Give yourself some time. Cream won't sag.

Let's make some diabetics. Cut that sugar
bag, drop it hot. Add some bay leaf (San Fran
or Chesapeake). In exile like this Aunt
of aunties? Hon, talk that fat free talk, canned

isolation, complexion just a touch,
a dash of fetish—Child! Can't put too much.

2.

But truth is, an old married couple, left
alone, resolves nothing. Just keep kicking
each other in their sleep. Recipes and Cooks
get this way. Cities and citizens get
this way. Shit, God and all creation too.
I recall getting kicked out the kitchen,

but my sister didn't. Worse than a whuppin'
where you pulled the switch yourself. Now these gaps
I got in the cookbook. Filé gumbo?
No. Old Fashioned red beans? No. Bunch of worn
down dishes, whipped up on the cheap.
Can still fry a bird golden, and say for grace
"The Kingdom of Heaven is at hand."
with a straight face. Bite and believe, again.

3.
Naturally. Squeeze the tail and suck the fat
from the head. Then throw the shell away.
What could be better than the whole damn day
boiled and seasoned? Ce bon, ce bon, in fact
see that house there? A new family, but don't speak
nothing but Yat. Recipe for a fight,
you ask me. Remember Gentilly nights
full of old Buddy Bolden hits and heat?

Gone. Oh, and that house on Paris and Pratt,
storm took that and another off Mandeville.
Copper got stolen too. For sure, I sat
and watched them strip. Man drove a Coupe de Ville
for thieving. A throwback. Could have been worse.
God could have sent us another white hearse.

• SONNET FOR THE SIDE EYE •

The storm is unimpressed with moans, your lack
of music. Can you match her tambourine
of rain, hail, her baritone sax called CAT (5),
her horn mute of cumulonimbus seen

for days, silencing the sun? The storm doesn't
bat an eye if your name is New Orleans
or Houston or heaven or play cousin,
you're gonna get this blue by any means

suitable to sweet, sweet Creole Kate. Shrew
untamed for sure. She treats you like a trade.
Say her name, say her name, then forget who
asked. No one's listening. Call a spade a spade

and a storm. How utterly human, true,
this envy for maelstrom to be like you.

• UNMASKING THE CHORUS •

July doesn't beg. The cicadas are coughing
through their tymbals and couldn't care less
whether anyone dreams of wings.

Acquire a husk they hum
like a cigarette hums alone in an ashtray
(tree?), a sound that stretches like the skin

of a snare drum. Dunce.
Abandon has its own bandwagon
and the confederacy of late summer's heat
can't assuage. Boredom. The horizon

sighs like a churchwarden pipe. *I could die
on this tree* the cicadas sing,
coughing themselves rare and blue
like a husk of song, the lyrics but not the tune.

• CREOLITE II •

Shape your mouth to say cousin
            or
                        ooh child
or
            to water at melon
            -

Slim your mouth to click after clique
            or
                        to say bad chicks
                                    & cold drink
say fuck like
                        me with mouth

fashioned after fisherman's hook

Lips bench
            press & part
                        to say double
dutch

Fix your mouth to mouth Gentilly
                        filé
                        play boy

Tune your mouth to
                        unmuted   trombone

• WHY ARE G-PHI MEN SO TOUGH? •

for Booker T. Washington H.S., Houston, TX
for the GENTS, a high school club in the model of black fraternities

Cue the band. The Baby Ocean of Soul's
horn section and drumline erupt. A tuba
talks out the side of its neck.
A bass licks the stage clean. DJ Screw
hooks the hardwood nude. In the wings, neophyte

GENTS answer *it must be the way we move,*
an augury, an entrance, geometric
slide, and a boot's gravity, the hard heel
contrapuntal baritone or a thunder

god closeted in a high school auditorium.
Even the dust can't keep its seat.
Booker T's step-team jumps and claps

under the thickest part of the thigh
then dips low, shooting hands across
the pelvis smooth as bow work across the bridge
of a cello. They syncopate to Salt-n-Pepa—*Get up*

on this. The routine ends in crescendo,
paused breath beading on lips, while young
men regiment to perfect

rows like an abacus. Soon an abdominal count
on everyone's mind, staring down the autumnal maroon
on boys' uniforms. The band becomes a sluice gate
for outro music, knocking the frames of civil rights

leaders off the wall. *Pistol Grip Pump* on trumpet
makes a clockwork swag, sets off a party line
dance and the GENTS begin imitating Alphas,
older brothers, and there is no rhetoric as dark

as their bodies. The wild applause booms back.
All this before the homeroom bell or a pencil
sharpener's crank heralds the school day.
These boys rest in a dialectic: their funk
against death, the body's drum tuned tight, a music

made of laying hands on oneself.
We so smooth, be the only prayer.

• LEARNING TO GAMBLE IN GRADE SCHOOL •

First a dreidel spun among blue public
school cots, where the petals of pencil shavings fell.

Next, clay's lesson: *Shin* meant put one in.
My black face didn't fade among my classmates.

Akin to dice against the schoolhouse brick,
a game to make knees ashy, hearts sick, and no one

aware I was the mixed kid in a gang of five
boys, only one of us was Jewish. *A great miracle*

happened there under the alphabet strip
weathered like God's own finger—only He could write

on the walls. Early readers and early gamblers we'd palm
sweets, eat and eat again the cooing brown

off chocolate coins, offer that teetotum
to its tiny whirlwind, and beg for *Gimmel*

all our lives. Our hands were dry as chalk
or a parted sea. Unabashed I warned Mama

someone ate the brown off the Jews, my eyes
like two burning bushes, her shrug like heaven's

indifference. I'd learn years later, my ancestors
ruled and razed the south of Spain but nothing of the living

Torah remains in me. I can hardly pronounce *Sephardic*.
Those morning school announcements left us dead

on our feet, coughing up the pledge of allegiance,
worse than the dreidel's open face to my face saying *Nun*.

• FAT •

Tuesday, much glitter
filling the gutter, parade
through some Zulu, carnival king,
beloved drunk with his drunk mother,
river teasing the city with its obesity,
the whole damn Gulf dyed purple

as a bruise on the thigh, backside
round as hallelujah in the mouth,
handsome cab, Gud Whiskey
poured in the ear, a dance reduced
to the bend in a beaux's wrist that says yes,
blessed black eye given

to the bigot, sea of plastic beads,
revelry after the club closes, that way
the Quarters club the air with music,
beat on a beat on a beat,
Gumbo pot filled to the top,
Po'boy longer than your arm,

Mema's house on a cinder block
quatrain, darkness fat as ham-hock,
that new world fleur-de-lis
stamped on the back of fool's gold, Easy
gone big, a saint with the other saints
amassing at the only Matins that matter—

the trumpet player bending a minor scale
until it's penitent   then making sin,
the Yat some speak, an unteachable accent,
dancing a second line across the teeth, the garrulous
polyglot Gulf seductive as the Aegean, triptychs
in Zydeco's bassline long enough to write

the epics that won't console, a lip-smack
left cold on a stranger's breast, or a field
of Elysium but really just a street
running through New Orleans
along bones layered with neighborhood
fat and hungry bulldozers, a parade

down to Lent, asking of God
what's He giving up, that time
He said *this city* and everyone
laughed, lifting their feathered masks
to kiss the night that ends
in Wednesday's ash.

• WHEN I FEEL A WHOOP COMIN' ON •

for the feast of Whitsuntide & After-Pschool Dances

ain't the butter
        fly, it's the tootsee
roll the speakers
        pose as a polemic
against your narrow hips

        this circle's musk
classmates grinding like
        black pepper in a cheap mill—
uneven, coarse. Shamelessly
        you practice outside

the arc of polo shirts, crop-
        tops and starchy jeans sharp
enough to cut penumbras
        from 8th graders. Summon
an adolescent faith to push

        past the girl who laid her tongue
in your mouth like a lisp on a field
        trip to the zoo, right
in front of the rhino
        exhibit. Your lonely Afro-
Latino blood bids

the center of hype,
ooooh, and funk to be
        filled with your inheritance—
flat feet, a skinny boy's sense
        of rhythm, and a soft uptown fade.

Go boy, Go
        you've only heard
in church. This dance is
        different than the holy
ghost shout filling half

        an hour on Sunday
nothing like the body
        rock of your father's bachata
he'd pull out to prove men
        with flat asses could dance.

Still you press and press
        throw your knees like bolos
catch up to the dj's scratch in
        time for the song to switch
choruses—Boyz II Men: *don't wait*

        till the water runs dry. Those
violins still weep for the awkward

slow drags you'll soon try
but there's a two second panoply
        where you've imitated the other

boys in their non-buttered fly
        in their roll tout-suite. There
at least a hip moment of locomotion
        where no one could charge
you with a lack of blackness.

        To the left, to the right
more flame than Pentecost,
        eyes like two upper rooms
wholly ghosted, your body
        becoming a tongue, spoken.

• ARS POETICA WITH ZYDECO •

"Leaving New Orleans also frightened me considerably."
—*John Kennedy Toole*

1.

What the sea laments is return
self to self; a tenderness.

Nobody dies here because no one goes
in the ground. We are not made wafers
for the mud's immeasurable tongues.

Communion rather is how I place—
my brown mouth on another brown mouth
not kiss, rather accent, this too—

a reaching sea returning to lament.

2.

The dead must rest
above ground or every last rite
would be a sea burial, our French

broken. The Gulf has always been
a great pall bearer.

We imbibe silence in white surf,
spit libation, lick, beg this Creole
walk water, raise dead, speak storm, then

remember our mouths
were made empty mausoleums—
even this Mississippi ends in toothless grin—

oh! What spirits are willing come
quick, quick, slow our tender meter

rises as tide on the edge of a tongue
making each bent utterance baptism.

3.
The poet says *a sea of grief is not a proscenium.*
I watch a pelican dive for two fish
hidden in the worn buoy's shadow. Who can tell
which lived its miracle to multiply, and which slid down
the pelican's gullet? If not a stage then what, poet?
I've exhausted the names for God's mirror. Let me had been.
I can only repeat myself. Amen, amen, amen.

2.

UNDER THE WIG I WORE CORNROWS

"…the scene was set; it repeated what / Was in the script / Then the theatre was changed…"

—WALLACE STEVENS, "OF MODERN POETRY"

"It is, contrary to the myth, an old, old struggle."

—LORRAINE HANSBERRY, "THE SCARS OF THE GHETTO"

• FEVER DREAM WITH MUSLIN FLATS
& ATONAL HUM •

The absolute fat lipped edge of the pitch
colored stage floor, a place to bow low
in the applause-less dark, to be in some field
left fallow, a stank on the breeze from bodies
and cut sugar cane. Later, shotgun
riding in a powder blue Coupe de Ville,
top down at the ass-end of ocean,

Stevie Wonder's high tenor shaking
static off the FM. Memory's stagecraft:
movable flats. Field again, men brown
as a violin's chest plucked by midday sun
strung from sycamore long enough to peel,
a method of acting like bark. Eyes open
like empty hammocks but still sweating,

as if waiting for music, as if waiting
for someone offstage to ask them to dance.
Who will come to strike this scenery? What dust
will remain in the rafters? What scrap of song will
knock feverishly against the perfect pitch dark?

• HEDLEY WITHOUT THE ROOSTER •

Here go the money, I heard Buddy
Bolden say, but forget it, today

it's just Dad wadding up a few twenties
to throw at my chest. *What you came for,*

take it away. A clump of double sawbucks
dropped where he taught two sons

to shoot hoops, welcome the sun as kinfolk,
dribble-drive, cross-over, drop-step, lay-up.

On a driveway nearly gone to weeds,
in heat that'd make an Oreo blister, backing me down

near the backboard he'd say, *Not a black man,*
an American, and scoop his baby hook. An easy two.

His strip of concrete, his court, and nothing made him miss
my mother more than asking for money. It came to trash

talk after every basket. Never beat him
head to head, the way he beat me

with bills. *Ever heard a young rooster dead*
in the middle of the night crow and wait?

Ever seen a man slaughter the king
of the barnyard? I waited all weekend

to ask, or crow, or beg some cash
for school clothes. What I got was a sternum

double tap, the blunt end of a macheted sunset,
an easy two. *Funky butt, Funky butt take it…*

Should've said more, backed him down, before
squatting at the crumbled curb,

my hand hooked into a beak, scooping
forty dollars off the ground…*away.*

Even confused, even in darkness, I hear the rooster
crow a command to the sun, saying rise,

and believe it. I hear Buddy Bolden in a dream,
his voice like fogged dawn, say, *Here go the money,*

and there is my father offering his hook shot to the sky.

• PLAYING BYNUM •

"I had the Binding Song. I choose that song because that's what I seen most
when I was travelling ... people walking away and leaving one another."
—Bynum, *from* Joe Turner's Come and Gone *by August Wilson*

The role required my dreadlocks
cut away. A short stump
of hair sprayed to gray. Imagine

this mock senescence
during prom season, with Clutch
City's teens half crazed with pomp

and circumstance. What benediction
on high school could I offer
other than Delilah's blessing?

Such was sacrificed
on altars of one-act play
tournaments in Texas. Our club

advisor called us Thespians:
some Greek for the sons
and daughters of Houston proper.

We were the color of olives
and Big Moe sipped purple
drank on the radio. Irrepressible,

smooth as the electric slide
at a family reunion, we funked
our jubas through after-school

practices, ran lines, lied
about sex, penned our names
to the auditorium brick. *c/o 2001*

I'd been hustling my stubborn
mules of respect for four years
through months of Saturdays

at suburban schools, acting
a plum fool across cafeteria
tables, coursing a beat

with *Bic* pens and a hard palm.
From the first years, I took
requests. Smack talk became

our digging root
work. Magic enough
for a summons. Our proud

ritual of parents drifted
into award ceremonies gentle
as censers swung at a mass.

Speech and drama against forgetting
when we failed—an empty seat
marked reserved. Bind 'em

just like glue the script said,
Joe Turner's come and gone
the script said, but we all knew

folks no older than us
still were shackled and snatched
for doing nothing in public.

And among those vagrancies
we stuck to sorrow's wall
like a slapdash poster labelled

coming soon.
Our adolescence paltry
as fish and loaves.

Our inherited boarding
house, where nothing shines
like new money, and cut hair

ain't nothing but wearing the wig
of the wind. We couldn't bind
what don't cling,

a curtain calling
our mispronounced names.
No matter how often

we circled, crossed
arms, held hands and bowed
our heads, we remained profane.

• RUTHERFORD SELIG STOPS FOR GOSSIP IN GREEN COUNTRY •

Local rumor claims every tree
is an immigrant. 'Course, no
one would say it to your face.

Folks sooner swallow a bullet
or blaspheme than admit anything
wrong with creation.

Surely Tulsa sits at the edge
of God's own chaise lounge,
the dammed Arkansas River

runnin' down the city's thigh
like a seam in a stockin'
and breezes get hot as a mole

on the Devil's ass, make
rust-red mud rise
firm as griddle cakes.

Some dish dirt that oil derricks
arouse the earth-toned men. I can't
rightly say. Day fat with sun,

midnight like a starvin' crow
perched on horizon, preaching
the Good Book: evenin' and mornin'

and it was good. Here is land as land is
rarely seen. Heard the Muskogee whisper
desolation without desert, many fields

and few lilies to consider.
Even the old bats stuck in walnut rockers
know plain tough grass twists to stubble

on a hill's chin and a dawn lathered in rain
gives way to lightning and fire
stiff as a straight-razor shave.

To mention weather is next to godliness.
Got a tornado horn that'll take a year
off your life. What a rush: one hard freeze

will bring a curse of black
ice to your lips. Snow on tribal casinos glows
neon and the bible schools illuminate the text on billboards.

In fall, black-splotched geese slant
the sky, a clear matte sky, hung the same
as dryin' linen. All the while the moon's pinched

light holds like God's own clothespin.
Night throws us under the revival tent.
And if folk can be believed

the dead are raised
in rumor. There are no graves we won't exhume.

PLAYING PROCTOR

"...and there is promise in such sweat"
          —John Proctor, from The Crucible *by Arthur Miller*

Given this ruddy, straightened wig no one could place
my face on a spectral scale of "ethnic." I slid

on and off stage. I spoke plain. I didn't name names. Some
audiences mistook me for Muscogee Creek. I spoke

in first person. Under that wig I wore cornrows
in Oklahoma's emaciated winter.

Arthur Miller was writing about hysteria
which can sound like tepid applause. Inside

the theater, the set was minimal: an askew
cross, brown flats mimicking wood. Our acting voices

restrained with Puritan diction. Everything seethed.
Nothing was faithful least of all the weather. *Goody*

was defined in the script. The wind outside mobbed the building
like a pack of crows. I witnessed daily the end

of the American Plains, after removing the stage
makeup and this wig. On the marquee of a washbasin

shaped convention center, another man of God
come to town. 50 years before, Miller whet his thumb

and now his lines are in my mouth. "Common vengeance
writes the laws." A lead role. We left realism in

the 19ᵗʰ century and look what remains. We
wanted a straight play about paranoia.

But outside the theater: horizon's bloody
lip, a monostich, the needle in a poppet.

• ULYSSES AS A NEGRO-BIRD •

Enduring the nor'easter, a bluebird enters
a half-town, a coda
resolving the Finger Lakes. Evening

gnaws on the damp bone
horizon until nothing's left,

but some gray
snow smeared like ash
on the forehead of door after door.

Bird of constant
sorrow, blue-black, half-blind, puffed with rain,
profile of shadow perched on a stuttering

branch, bird with his song taut
as bowstring, flattens notes

across peeled sycamore bark, shivering
to name again
the final island. Home,

Home. By dawn
his hours sung are not
enough. The day's firstborn

light reveals what hasn't survived.
Not even a dog left to remember.
No one waits for a wailing.

A rabid wind
greedy as Scylla eats six
notes from the scale leaving

this shrill-as-a-whistling-
arrow-piercing-the-air flat-note
caught in the bird's throat. Locals exiting

the half-town truncate all naming
down to, "I am… I am…" A sliver of
lightning renews the town's burning bush.

Bleating begins in the streets. The sun blinks,
then blinds itself with a fog. The bird's shadow,
hung from a tree, burns in effigy.

• SUPREMACY •

Consider the shuttlecock
its deft lightness, its rubber nose
unbent, its attention to racket,
its fear of the ground, its willingness
to lob or smash, its whiteness, its penchant
for being held
afloat by the slightest breeze and histories
of swing, how it needs to be
batted between two players,
how it recognizes their want;
consider its feathers, its plastic, its conical
shape suggesting hierarchy, and always
its weight in your hand, how it seeks to be served.

• ANTI-CONFESSIONAL I •

This poem will inherit the earth.

Flame on the forehead;
palm oil on both palms.

A preacher anoints a nightstand:
try not to balk. Like a ventriloquist

the poem repeats
without opening its mouth.

This poem wore a conk
slicked through its adolescence

and caught a generation of conch
shells to make creole for hotel guests

and tourists. This poem loves tourists
about as much as a clean, fingernail

colored shore, which can erase
only their footprints and not

their eczema of plastics. This poem
has an empty passport, has registered

to vote left and obsesses
over ephemera. The poem self

publishes and declares all deities
dead, except the writers

of the apocryphal gospels.
Every poem can only go down

in flames, so this poem auditions
for cancelled TV shows

In Living Color
and *Living Single.*

The poem cleaves
a black lamb for covenant

and calls it a lucky break
beat. The poem arrives late

in life, unable to comfort,
unable to speak.

• ABUELITO •

Rubbed clean like callouses
on a praying hand, the office floors
my grandpa mopped from sundown
to some hell-bent hour held an obstinate shine.

His patron saint: the bald domestic,
Mr. Clean. Grandpa scrubbed his tongue
with a Brillo pad of commercial jingles,
turned TV into a cheap tutor. Weekly

bouts with his wife Dolores dulled
his shrine of woodgrain & cathode ray tube,
but not his stare. *Where were you*
last night? What news of San Pedro Sula?
Did you buy the plátanos?

Many fly-swatting afternoons
he'd sit with his boxers around
his ankles into early evening
smelling the oblivion of his own funk,
touching and imagining himself a papí
chulo. Atlacatl, his name

like the crank of an engine,
a name with grease in the gears,
same as his brothers,

the name of a conquistador
resistor, one he could not clean,
donning instead Carlos, the name he'd given
his son like a disinheritance, his own
poco colonización. Another version of mixing
a little dirt from Europe with the mashed plantains.

• ODE TO PATRICK STEWART
SNATCHED BY MAMA •

Playing captain on TNG you brought sexy
back to balding, or so my mother said
half-smacking her lips on *Jean-Luc*, easy
on brown eyes that never loved white

men before. All those roles in the RSC
prep to sit on the set, Roddenberrian
throne leathered in late 80s tan.
Among your stage credits: Nobility caught

in a photo negative stage production—*Othello*.
Gray temples fully shaved, blackface rubbed out
the imaginary cast list, dark love
calling back the days when you lived

in my living room TV, making mulattos
in my mother's mind, her Desdemona
fantasy, and true she doesn't even know
that name, but could pull it off

pull down the world's stage or at least undress
taboos, having bowed before in one Minnesota
courthouse, near Mankato State, newly pregnant,
newly married, with you she could do this

as quickly as she's taken over this ode.
Sir Patrick Stewart, the one of my memory
way back when two TVs could stack
on each other, alternative shelves,

you were loved not wisely but too well.

• ODE TO LANDO CALRISSIAN •

If you were stuntin' in a galaxy far, far away, blue cape
suave, with a gold lining that would shame the sun
with a cool walk and a gambler hustle,

if you had a hair style so fresh, you'd claim
to have won it off an out-of-work cloud
city cosmetologist, if even your eyebrows

had scoundrel in their arch, if everybody knew
the music bumped cargo hold to cockpit in the Millennium

Falcon, a name straight out of P. Funk,
if everyone could see those hands churning
the dark dream of stars into the buttermilk

of a hip brother running his own city,
if we asked, *where are all the black people
in the galaxy?* Would you help us? Would you bet on us?

• ODE TO RHONDA •

for my mother

Diastole of memory, new blues given simply: a blue
street lamp beating dangerous block, beating bored police,
beating a goodbye fist against all front doors. *What if* this
city, this Baltimore in the imagination was her home town?
Pop music made an oracle of her name *Help me, Rhonda.*
*Help, help…*as much a sonata as dawn light on the dew.
Some moments music cannot score: her daddy shot,
whiskey fresh on his breath, TV set in his arms, half
sprawled out a window. At eleven she could teach blue
to Matisse, pose like a nude cleaning Sunday greens. Come
twenty had a way of walking that'd make eyeballs sweat,
stirring on sidewalks the way red beans stir in a pot.
O Rhonda, we all need help remembering grace.

• SHERLOCK EXAMINING THE TABLE OF AUNT ESTER •

1.
Mahogany table, circa 1948, Orwellian
design—inset seismograph and cathode
ray tube slung below like an automaton
hog belly—translucent surface on top.

Legs hewn as elongated tent spikes,
"The earth is a man's head Judges 5:24"
carved down the left edge. Sufficient
home altar. Chalk and blackboard

catalogue above hand blown glass jars:

Orris root suspended in sea water, cork
sealed tin of pigeon urine, beet blood,
Solomon seed, buckeye, and bone dust.
A row for Ogun: mandrake, squill, and rum

to promote iron in the blood and erection.
Many vials smeared with red mud. All the dark
wood doused in orthodox incense and ori oil,
its scent creolized with an odor of burnt yucca.

Table trim notched to count moon phases.
Hygiene of its own: human hair knotted
to dread—some ginger, brunette, and kink—
tied over bronzed handles. A single drawer.

Accent of hyacinth twisted with ribbon, a touch
of woman. Twin bells ringing thin at a slight brush.

2.

Lady of the house roused to the room, near dead
blunt tucked in her lips' left corner, the trail of two
foot dreadlocks, tied up, stirred the shadowing smoke.
Mistress sans master, matched to the mahogany table,
textures equal, pocked with moles twinning the black
heads of vials. Seems she birthed, body and soul,
this dark wood, but for the disparate skin. Today she
casually palms a mango. Tomorrow a fresh skull. Imagine
no difference in her gait or expression whichever gets tossed
and caught like a bored child. *Now what'cha be needin'* dropped
in the ear slow as spit. Adequate hush without remedy.
And without stutter I began, "Orris root suspended in sea…"

• EDMUND DANTÈS DRINKS GRAPPA WITH FREDDIE GRAY •

"All human wisdom is contained in these two words—Wait and Hope"
—Alexandre Dumas, The Count of Monte Cristo

You know what I want on my gravestone?
Only the dead leave the Chateau d'If.
I'd leave my sons a ritual of self-portraits
done year by year at the cemetery

the Monte Cristo Gold lining their teeth.
Merde! If these sons weren't wisps of wasted grappa
pooling in a mind's cracked flask.
We need a gallows humor for the presumed dead.

I'd have the reaper wearing the new clothes
of the emperor, naked as the coroner's slab after a body.
Salut! And you, for your sons? You'd leave
them what? A hashtag? A sneaker's ash

from burning off at first sight. Come, come
I can't even sleep in a bed anymore.

You went to the hospital; I went to the sea. *Only*
the dead leave the Chateau d'If.
Here's to the privilege of shooting a breeze.
Here's to sons that are only a breeze.

60

You know I didn't scream for Mercedes
as much as you think. Let's line up the shots:
one for every minute in leg irons, and let's see
one for your spine, one for my destitute father

whose hungry belly and broken heart hung him
from the rafters of despair. Certainly, one for that
dear sister of yours, who must forever speak
your full name to strangers. She will never see

the Catalans or the Isle of Elba as you do now
ghosting the world through t-shirts and picket signs.

• CEREMONIES IN DARK OLD MEN •

1.

I linger on
shit like a fly
in summer

with a vaudeville
of whiskey, my hair
smooth

as an arrow's
fletch. I play
the dozens

on this porch,
mince oaths, take
the high

yellow epithet
my half brother
blurts

out after *King
me.* I tell him
you black

enough to be
back of a wolf's
mouth.

2.

I been
an unkinged red
checker

been top dog
and underdog, clap
in a juba

and the boot's
stomp, been a day
of absence

been half brother
and play cousin
been savage

on a blues riff,
a capella my whole
life, been black

as half this board,
been sour mash
bottled

fermented like folk
song in the oak
barrels.

• PLAYING LEVEE •

"That's what you is. That's what we all is. A leftover from history."
—Toledo, from Ma Rainey's Black Bottom *by August Wilson*

The white drama
teacher pits my friend William
and me against each other: two trains
running on the same track.
We master our instruments
of silence and embrace
when cast into roles. We are told
to let our tongues stutter
like a graveled road.

One…two…you know what to do

we brothers
so we bandstand
among hallway lockers:
intervals of gold then blue.
Three entrances
of sneer, sex, and swag
William carries to our school
auditorium, lifts his script
from a back pocket. Auditions.
I follow like a rumor.

I want to see the dance you call the black bottom

I keep
the character with a name
built as an embankment
to prevent a river's overflow.
William slips his voice
into Toledo, a piano player,
his gap-tooth smile
a black key. My hands
palm a brass horn. We begin
to finger the valves
of seventeen

I want to see the dance you call the big black bottom

We are told,
by Aunties and O.G.s, every decade
in the 20th century, the blues
begets again Ma Rainey's
bottomless alto, dignifying
a minor scale, bending radio
waves round the ears of August
Wilson, shining the Florsheims
of hope until a boy can see
himself and his friend
when he hangs his head.

It puts you in a trance

and there at the top
of memory's spit-polished shoe
William's face and fresh cut
his skin's recursive black
a singularity, like beauty
compressed to its darkest
inside the mouth of a trumpet.
His beauty like a one man band.

It puts you in a trance

All the lines for Levee
lead my switchblade
through my friend's belly
as cool and laconic
as muted trumpet.
The script calls
for a backstab up to the hilt
but we ignore
this, tilt and embrace instead
chest to chest.
Our drama teacher claps
his offbeat praise.
There is nothing to say,
over a lost love

and loved brother.
What becomes
of a man's song
when there is no record?

You ought to learn that dance

• LAURELS & THUNDER •

1.

A prelude to practicing our suplexes and top rope
dives, The Giant & Hogan duking it out on the tube,
I rested in a headlock, as my brother forgot his grip
and slouched on the couch. Here the blond Hulk
stood framed between our old set's wood grain,
staring up Andre's long black unitard. Some night.

A Slam! Course, rumor was The Giant was all ruse.
Threw the fight and let Hogan lift him. I nearly exploded,
my brother shouting, "Hot damn!" over and over,
his hand on my head like laurels, and our difference
in age disappeared and stayed gone for years. A comfort,
since I stumbled behind him on the basketball court, so long
staging myself in his costumes: a letterman, a high-top fade,
a neck strung with drama club medals: duet acting. But enough.

What I want to say is I've mixed up so much, but that slam
remains, body and all, ruse or real and everything else is
lists of groceries, drool on church pews, piles of debt letters,
minutia of rain on roof, the winter's erasure,
births, deaths, and so much blues without music.

2.

So. Saturday mornings, our hands on the vertical hold
dial, twisting the flickering image between the wood-

grain, we ate Frosted Flakes and sang the Thunder-
Cats theme song, shouting *hooooooo*, with wonder

in each other's face. My godlike older brother and I
arguing over who'd be Panthro, over whose black eye

was coming first. Sight beyond sight is what we learned
as our dad demanded a divorce, and shouted *Holy shit I've earned*

this at our mother. I understood I couldn't hate him. More-
over I loved my brother. O my beautiful older brother, how sore

your left cheek slapped by our white-hot summers
between parents. The years after, how you learned to turn the other

to the world, your hands on the vertical hold of love
gone wrong. I want a theme song for your pain. Bruh

I want the thunder and rain, and you to be a panther
again. Lovely, dark, dangerous, and wild as heat lightning.

• RHAPSODY IMAGINING THE SOUND AND FORM OF A DRIBBLE •

Rapid pace. Lebron fleeced on a drive
to the basket, reminds me. Five
past eight in a small bar,
a small town. Drinking hard
& dry cider alone. I watch a mute
television screen, flash and shoot
replayed to the clink of clean glasses
on the bar. Where are my brother's lashes
of bravado and his pantomime of black
joy: broad smile, a gleaming shack
of teeth? I hear him in a palm
slapping the maple wood counter to song
"Get back on D!" but really that's me
shouting at the LEDs.
Such a small comfort to remember
his voice, exuberant, uncouth, fuller
than bellows at a hot forge.
The TV's unflinching of course
in the midsummer buckling heat.
Screen after screen where guards meet
a center to fight thru. Perhaps a law
slight enough, worthy and raw,
is to roll, roll
towards whatever basket of cold
pleasure an evening provides

in a cigarette shared as a stranger lies
back in a lingering smoky smile,
to show you've not grown too wild
& fat to spark against
the flint of another's desire. Repentance
unrequired. Just a smile though, roll
roll towards whatever cold
basket of pleasure a marriage
provides. The erotic familiar. Leverage
of scent in the sheets, a hint
of smile, an elixir bent
towards youth. Such a small
comfort to remember love at all
persistent as a 7-foot center
crashing the boards, after
missing an easy lay-up. Nothing is
as large as what is
not said to a beautiful
woman, a beautiful man, or the comfortable
hills smoking themselves
in a passionate lightning, or even the well
meaning sun sinking in a basket
you can't see, but know, fantastic
as it seems, is larger than any cold
common pleasure towards which we roll.

• HOW OUR SONS LEARNED TO FIGHT •

The same chest-thumping tableau
of two men disrobed and so close
their fears thin to apple skin.

We ain't hear nothing. Drum kit,
we forget whose breath broke
the silence. In the dark

can anyone tell one groan
from another: the angel's
or Jacob's, or the subwoofer

praying hard to our knees,
which fall and rise, unrepentant,
to the parquet floor? The punchbowl

gloriously shatters, slapped
with strobe light. Our bodies
remember our fathers

saying throw the first fist
and buck. We remember
we invented our fathers'

advice about how to fight
another man, because we
did not know how to begin

a love, only how to bruise the end.

• BLAME •

And it came like a wet pig
snout seeking the brush for the last truffle,
the growing gnaw that you were not
good enough. You did not have an Atlantic

to cross. You did not have a trauma
anyone was buying. Your tongue grew
banal as a calm sea. Eyes you dreamed
were artillery have had their hoods

drawn over. You weren't worthy of a stray
bullet. In the fitfully coy Maryland
winters you saw an unused sepulcher.
You thought of the cut marble

the pallbearers slid your grandmother in.
You thought of licking the bacon grease
from a used pan when the fridge was barren.
You thought of playing spades on the hood
of a car, and losing a few books, going blind.
Nothing was to blame

but your own imagination. You have
no place to comeback from. No one calls
it a comeback, when you start from the bottom

and return, like a muddy nose that can't stop
sniffing the pot of cleaned greens and hocks
cooking for the New Year.

How many years without a single black
eyed pea, before the ancestors cease
to weep? How many entrails must you eat?

3.
Leaving the Panopticon

"The actor is / a metaphysician in the dark…"
—WALLACE STEVENS, "OF MODERN POETRY"

"I am a wind from nowhere. / I can break your heart."
—AI, "THE KID"

• ANTI-CONFESSIONAL II •

The poem says, *I've been made up*

like a Mardi Gras mask. A purple feather.
History's glitter. A slot for each eye.

Like Divine in the dressing
room trailer, humming *Good Morning
Baltimore*.

Like any body
lifted by its own
bootstraps. An ascension lies on the sky.

The poem announces, *All suffering*

must end and proceeds
into the afterlife of metaphor.
There is still a door.

The poem asks the dead *where
have you gone?* then raps
its knuckles on a desk.

• THE INNER HARBOR'S OCTAVE •

for C.

The only incorruptible sight here is the green of the camphor tree,
its rhizomes in your iris, extracting an oil. Scent on the wind raises

a Lazarus kiss we shared one harbor side afternoon, the algae
blooms hidden for once below the water's skin of sunlight.

The pig-iron colonial cannons all facing away. The horizon
unable to show any embarrassment, blushes hours after

we've left the hill, left it verdant and clinging to the gossip of cicadas.
Green is the color of cleaving. It has wrestled Eros from red.

• SLAB •

August has exhausted
the rain's celibacy
and I loaf on my bone-colored
porch, the muted evening

hues waving back
on the backs of black
ants willing to rot inside
a day-old plantain's husk.

My son's heel
comes to crush
this splotched temple
crusted over with a sweet

spit and each stiff
thorax throbbing.
Some die with sugar
rimming their mouths.

I lift my son's heel bruised
black with dead ants;
the plantain's musk
has masked us both,

so cleaning his sole
flat, slow with
a folded dish rag must
look to those fifty ellipsis

still rejoicing
in smeared fruit
like a sky becoming
a mass grave.

Or something indecent:
annunciation
in a thunderhead
                broken.

The rain relents, falls
the ants retreat
like an unstrung rosary
my son sits on his portion

of porch, curses
his feet, curses me,
curses the dead
ants he can't bring back.

• THE BROKEN JUG •

after William Merritt Chase
for Tsunade

Look, sweet one, how she is obeying
a bargain not to be still life,

how she's been posed on the verge of speaking
yet kept silent; I don't wish this for you.

Look, here the artist abandoned alabaster
for an earthen jug, simple clay, the color of us,

and the hills behind nearly bruised to black
set on horizon as if in the past

we must remember. Knuckle on knuckle,
that's not the grasp of prayer. Her broken heirloom

that midwifed milk, wine watered down, whatever
drowns thirst, left on the road like a baby

doll after a war. Look, little one, how she will not
look at us. Unease on wooden shoes painted

a potato's yellow. She's never heard the word *bastard*
until a moment before dropping her jug. I imagine

her peeling potatoes down to white
while her father scrapes black ice

tobacco from his pipe, her mother dying
this scrap cloth a dull yellow

to wrap her newly rounded waist.
That wisp of headband redder than watermelon flesh.

• WALKING THE PANOPTICON •

after Robin Rhode

The scrape of my father's unshaven face
was my first love. Because of questions

my daughter asks while walking through the museum
Is that you? Daa-ddy is that you? All the men

in photographs, with skin the color of wet
wood, queried. I was mimicked

bone, sickle, a ringing
ear under glass that hears when I don't answer,

guarding the silence like Cerberus. We pause,
latched to a leash of dust, before

this ear, brown as filé powder.
My reflections smudge the archival glass.

I look back, she looks back. My father is light
as mango flesh. She leans on that light like a sail.

• THE INNER EAR •

"Something for your poetry, no?"
—*Carolyn Forché*, "The Colonel"

Forget listening. Consider each ear's cartography, .
its width of cartilage and lobe, curled dragons
guarding the skull's flanks.

Taut skin of hidden drums. Once a friend
lodged a green M&M inside one.
She dreamed a cockroach
would crawl in after. Plant flags

in the New World. Measure by measure.
What's the medical term for memory
loss? Once my brother was bathed

by a neighbor. He couldn't speak
for a week. I heard the water
stop running. I can't remember his face.

Whose? *What?* Whose? *I wasn't listening.*

• THE DARKROOM •

Alone at the coat check, handing over
the family's London Fogs and North
Faces I say *Enough*. Calipers

can't unscrew enough to measure
my son's naked smile when I ask
about Sumaya, the darkest child

in his class. He is only six, but turns
his face from mine to smile
wider. It's not what you think. A guilt

lingers on my eyelashes. He is only six
and already he's been told
he's not black. This vice unscrews

like calipers until the tips touch
me an ochre, a bone still dressed in gristle,
and him an ambrotype before the flash

the exposed, opaque parts relatively light.
Am I a fool to think that smile
my son can't show means he already loves

what it took me years to love? I wish for a mirror.
Would it be enough if his pleasure could hold
like balsam resin, if he could learn early

which hands come
to develop photographs of their own
horrors, and which come to wade

in the waters of a darkroom with tenderness?
And how the sun shutters so slow,
whatever moves in us is blurred.

• INDENTURED FIGURE •

I'd kill for a set of teeth. Whale, wolf, or sloth. I'd overlap them, make a hideous maw, and bite the walls behind me. I want a smile that says threat. I want a smile that speaks easy—a smile like a bluff, like refugees down a sea cliff. My eyes have grown metal pincers to measure the distance between quirks of hate. I can't shut them. Why else would I face this wall? I wear a hat made of white stone, it's heavy and stinks of bird shit. My neck is wrapped in a stranger's scarf. I bear it. Below my shoulders I'm as thin as an eyelash. Every toenail refuses to stop growing —they curl and laugh at me from inside the wall of my body. I can't leave. I can't eat. I'll make meat out of anything, even the air. Molar.

• LEAVING THE PANOPTICON: MY FATHER DOESN'T KNOW THIS ABOUT ME •

but he will. The reason I draw with both hands, the reason I forced myself to whistle, is for the fun of not knowing what to call myself. Every day in our black-box of a car, we play a game. He calls a name; I say white or black (sometimes brown). He repeats whatever I say. What I don't say is larger than what I do. When the museum closes, and those docent statues walk home, I sneak back and unhook all photographs from the eggshell walls. I spit on the hooks just to be close. My father won't care, like the men under glass care. They pronounce my name by naming colors.

• THE INNER HARBOR'S SESTET •

We've left. The hill verdant and clinging to the gossip of cicadas,
unable to show any embarrassment, blushing hours after.
The pig-iron colonial cannons face away. The horizon
blooms hidden for once below the water's skin of sunlight.
A Lazarus kiss. We shared one harbor-side afternoon with the algae
the only incorruptible sight here like the green of the camphor tree.

• ANTI-CONFESSIONAL III •

This isn't a secret; I have failed
to love with the patience of hibiscus root
whose buds bloom with no thought
of being tea. I have not loved
my innocence, overdressed in morning light.
How can the earth keep turning
to the thing that will kill it? Oh Sun,
bring me a warm hill in August,
an echo of a fragile and immortal green,
a better remembrance
of my grandma's eyes. I have failed
to forget love is one of many
higher choruses, and yes there are octaves
of light that linger. Can we still call love
love anymore? Or have we avoided failure?
Every ode must fail, if there is to be a higher love.

ACKNOWLEDGMENTS

I would like to thank the editors of the following journals where these poems first appeared (sometimes in a different form):

2 Bridges Review: "Ethel Cooking Béchamel," "Hedley Without the Rooster"

Baltimore Museum of Art Blog: "The Broken Jug"

The Baltimore Review: "How Our Sons Learned to Fight"

The Fiddleback: "Sherlock Examining the Table of Aunt Ester" under the title "Sherlock Examining the Table of Lady Walker"

Fledging Rag: "Ars Poetica with Zydeco," "Edmund Dantes Drinks Grappa with Freddie Gray," "Inamorata"

jubilat: "When I Feel a Whoop Comin' On"

The Nashville Review: "Creolite II"

No, Dear: "Slab"

Prairie Schooner: "Primer," "Ulysses as a Negro-Bird"

Queen Mob's Tea House: "Fat"

Scalawag: "Abuelito," "Playing Levee," "Rutherford Selig Stops for Gossip in Green Country"

Skelter: "Ode to Rhonda"

Vinyl: "Supremacy"

I am abundantly grateful to the members of the Washington Writers' Publishing House for selecting my book as the 2020 winner of the Jean Feldman Poetry Prize. Elizabeth Knapp, Nicole Tong, and Holly Karapetkova in particular gave attentive and insightful editorial guidance. I am so glad to be a part of the WWPH crew.

I want to specifically thank my dear friend and fellow poet, zakia henderson-brown. Without her steadfast friendship, intelligence, and belief in these poems I would have quit long ago. Thank you for helping me believe that the book was possible.

I owe a great debt to the poets Tim Seibles and Cynthia Manick, whose feedback and encouragement in the latter stages of development helped the manuscript find its soul.

Many thanks to the friends and family who supported me during the years it took to write this book. Some read early drafts and gave feedback. Some gave timely words of wisdom. Some simply kept their word when I needed it most. Thank you to Charif Shanahan, Bill Hoard, Anthony Moll, Joseph Ross, Evan Lesavoy, Kyle Erickson, Ann Marie Brookmeir, Alan King, Karl Henzy, Andrew Sargus Klein, Lynne Price, Marion Winik, Jane Delury, Betsy Boyd, Robin Coste Lewis, and Kyle Dargan.

Thank you to my teachers and mentors Valzhyna Mort, Ishion Hutchinson, Kendra Kopelke, and Stephen Matanle for teaching me the craft.

Many of these poems were written with the support of fellowships from the Vermont Studio Center and The Fine Arts Works Center in Provincetown, MA. And of course, eternal gratitude to Cave Canem, whose fellowship changed my life.

I also want to thank my parents and my dear brother, Rabu Leyva, to whom the book is dedicated. My brother was the first person to encourage the arts in my life. His model, his integrity, and his enduring humor are everywhere in this book.

To my children, Tsunade and Simon, I hope the poems in this book make you proud.

And thank you to Casey who keeps me believing in the highest love.

NOTES

Page 9: Swiss Confectionary is a famous cake shop in New Orleans.

Page 11: "Ear Hustle" in the final stanza references the song "Quick" by Tank and the Bangas, and the NPR Tiny Desk concert given by the band.

Page 31: The line *"a sea of grief is not a proscenium"* is from the poem "Notebook of a Return to the Native Land" by Aimé Césaire.

Page 36: The poem "Hedley Without the Rooster" references the character of Hedley from August Wilson's play *Seven Guitars*. In the play Hedley has a vision/dream of Buddy Bolden bringing him money. Buddy Bolden was a famous jazz musician in New Orleans in the late 19th and early 20th century. No known recordings of Bolden exist.

Page 42: Rutherford Selig is a character in both *Joe Turner's Come and Gone* and *Gem of the Ocean* by August Wilson. He is both a "people finder" and travelling merchant of odds and ends. He is one of three white characters in Wilson's ten plays.

Page 54: TNG is an acronym for Star Trek: The Next Generation. RSC is an acronym for Royal Shakespeare Company.

Page 60: Edmund Dantes is the unjustly imprisoned protagonist of Alexandre Dumas' *The Count of Monte Cristo*.

Page 62: The poem shares a title with *Ceremonies in Dark Old Men*, an American two-act play by Lonne Elder III.

Page 65: Florsheim is a brand of shoe, from a Chicago-based company founded in 1892. The shoe brand is mentioned several times in *Ma Rainey's Black Bottom* by August Wilson.

Page 80: The poem "The Inner Harbor's Octave" begins with a paraphrased line by Eugenio Montale from his poem "On the Llobregat," translation by Charles Wright.

CPSIA information can be obtained
at www.ICGtesting.com
Printed in the USA
LVHW091328201020
669297LV00001B/8